LOVE ME TENDER

Nick Papaxanthos

Mansfield Press

a stuart ross book

Library and Archives Canada Cataloguing in Publication

Papaxanthos, Nicholas, author

Love me tender / Nick Papaxanthos.

Poems.

ISBN 978-1-77126-093-0 (paperback)

I. Title.

PS8631.A639L69 2015 C811'.6 C2015-906205-5

Editor for the Press: Stuart Ross

Design & Typesetting: Stuart Ross

Cover Painting: Georgia Fullerton

Author Photo: Rachael Pasma

The publication of *Love Me Tender* has been generously supported by the Canada Council for the Arts and the Ontario Arts Council.

ONTARIO ARTS COUNCIL
CONSEIL DES ARTS DE L'ONTARIO
an Ontario government agency
un organisme du gouvernement de l'Ontario

Canada Council for the Arts Conseil des arts du Canada

Mansfield Press Inc.

25 Mansfield Avenue, Toronto, Ontario, Canada M6J 2A9

Publisher: Denis De Klerck

www.mansfieldpress.net

LOVE ME TENDER

CONTENTS

THE VACCINATED DAWN

WAKING UP

The right wall is bricks.
The left is cement
painted as bricks. The
right window is jammed
shut. The left is open,
full of voices. On the
floor, beside my bed,
a left slipper. My
left foot slips in. It's
morning, the right time
for breakfast, so I open
the drawer of cutlery
to my right. There is only
one spoon left, my least
favourite spoon, and
my right hand is the
spoon's least favourite too.
When I reach into my
bowl of cereal, the spoon
veers left, scooping
at the air, spilling milk
and sending the bowl
to the floor, smashing
over my slipperless right foot.
The pain goes right, left,
mostly up, but everywhere,
so I close my eyes.
Now everything
moves in my favourite

direction: no direction.
The pain moves there too,
but slowly, slowly,
as I settle into direction
again, eyes opening,
open.

AFTER THE BROKEN LEG

The wind snatches a plastic bag, a pattern
Waking up that fills in the blank
Where the puddle gives, lowering its ladder.

The bad timing, the curtsy, the yawn—
The curtsy rising through a funnel
When the door swings open over a sudden drop—

But now sleep comes off its dream,
Which is here, where the puddle is only a sea
And the flowers look down from further up
So whoever wants can take one.

SONNET TO A DREAMED HAND

I stand at the edge of a diving board.
Below, the pool boils. Steam rises
in thick, unwavering lines.
I reach out and they are like fingers.
One curls around my thumb,
another presses into my palm. I think
I am holding a hand—I think
this is what it's like to hold a hand.
I remember pulling someone to safety, squeezing,
and the hand slipping through.
I remember a patch of wet cement.
When you lie down on it,
you think your head is a pillow
and the ground is a head.

THE VACCINATED DAWN

A sink washes the air's hands
A detour around the candle darts
That plow into the wall of a flame
Scoring ten points for Team Dumbbell.

A trepanned sheep ignores all of this
But huge funnel shapes hold its breath
The drama narrowing to a single point
You poke with a stick.

IN TWO PARTS

I dialled the wrong number
but the right person picked up.

*

Now that you're covered in food
the table isn't.

LEARN BY DOING

Jane smacks Peter.
They wait in silence.
They pray together.
Jane stays in the tower
and becomes an urn.
Peter opens a drawer
filled with murders
in the attic-shaped light.
The trees escape their leaves.
The lake fights off the reflection
of a terrible bucket.

IN THE ALTAI REGION OF RUSSIA

Child

instead of

sausage

found

dead

mother

in fridge

CHAIRLIFT TO HELL

Dawn across the pyramid lawn
someone is trying to mow.

Barry New and the Scented Lotions
perform their hit single “Spank My Membrane.”

The tree grows up into a real table.

A collar pulls loose
from its pastel shirt
and fastens around
a flower’s throat.
The petals lounge
in the refurbished room,
reading magazines.

Frosty the Wheelchair
tackles a freckled boy
at the car wash.

Farms drool tractors.

Under the sea, no lamb bleats.
No lamb, no lamb.
And the speckled fish are not my friends.
Could never be.

Bananas go bald.
Yellow wire.

Lightning tiptoes
out of the sky's armpit
into summer's House of the Eyebrow,
which I pluck.
The windows shatter,
lightning gnashes the roof
then pokes its heads out
the sky's armpit again.

The Buffet Newlyweds
perform their hit single "Dismantle Grandma."

The freckle jogs a couple laps around my neck.

✐

Times when I looked and saw
a lizard in the soap dispenser,
small fires flattened into ancient coins,
tennis balls drop from the yawns
of professionals, and seeds kick up
their insides through a field
and look around.

✐

The eyes wander without a brain
to make sense of what they're seeing.

✐

The stars' eyes sweep their gaze
into a bright heap
under the snow-capped shoulders
of Big Joe.

✐

A folded shirt nailed to a wall.
A grilled cheese riddled with thumbtacks.

✐

Chest hair of the Swamp Thing.

Three grandmothers.
They were boys
who swallowed stuff
from little bottles.

Vitamins roll in,
eclipse the stars.

Times when I listened and heard
dishwater pulsing in the dust,
a sardine peeled off a hot sidewalk,
a hummingbird buzz through another,
splitting it in two.

The sky's immortal pregnancies,
rain poking birds, fat clouds—
Do you think of the emmenagogues?

The dinosaur roars and rapes a leaf.

PROPER TALE

Several doctors visited the field-guide photo in Japan
while the smoke-filled idiot cradled actual light in his arms.
The barbarians came in full undies from the lower regions
through the field of wood. Bikini-clad meter maids
licked along their bristly edges: “Keep the hair in!”
Their voices like jagged cream made them a target
for lightning. Eventually
we walked alone again, passing the story down
through tongueless generations. I sobbed
over the unpowered ear-engine of our culture
under the hollowed-out cabbage sunlight
in the dry wind in the mountain air in the city
until my thumb stuck out, and like a photocopy
unto infinity, hitched ride after ride
to where I’ll always be.

AFTER SOME NEW EUROPEAN POETS

Souvenir of Liège

The little square discharge of a window.

White Siestas

The shore is littered with camels.

After Luis García Montero

Water seduces the sandcastle,
revealing the king's missing tongue.

After Abdelwahab Meddeb

The squirrel scurried along the swan's neck.

Saison du Corps

A trail of teeth led me to your mouth.

After Urs Allemann

Your head slides off your shoulders
then bends you over to pick it up.

16 April 1994

A curtainless hush disables the wind.

After Chus Pato

The maiden paints the blue mushroom green
and lifts the curse on the milking machine.

São Pedro de Alcântara

The view stands up on its hind legs.

Star, Meteor, Some Shooting Thing

reloads the senseless night.

After the Rain

The Laundry Territories unfold their blue valleys.

After Elisabeth Wandeler-Deck

The desert's backflip lands the vultures.

In the Empty Hallway

The aquarium-like peace of your vomit.

Wrestling Lake

A pile of ripples weighs in at 19 pounds.

THIS WINDOW

This window looks onto a courtyard, a bag of peanuts.
This window is fastened with a seat belt.
This window pulls away from the wall like a puddle from the curb
towards a drain.
This window lets you reach through and flick pigeons like switches
in a cockpit.
The view recedes steadily from this window with a sound like
tuning a radio.
Two of these windows drool.
Clouds pass through a canyon reflected in an opposite window.
A pulse across the windowsill enhances the horizon.
My French sounds great from this window.
This window wheezes like a broken accordion.
You can blow bubbles through this window
but don't go near that window, squinting through its grime, its
fuck-ups and regrets.
The onlooking windows argue over metaphors for a shattered
window:
a collage peeled apart or a silent squadron of jets?
All at once, pigeons rise over the courtyard.
I flick them all at once.
A pigeon smacks my window.
Another falls to the courtyard then smacks my window.
I stick my head out the window and see David McFadden,
a tiny electrical storm brewing above his brain.
He throws a word at a window and it bounces off.
Sometimes a window is so clear, it consumes your field of vision,
but if you look out the same window every day, you might stall for
a moment.
Why are you so sad?

Maybe you never could fix that window.
Maybe you're planning to move.
Once you threw a paper airplane out your second-floor window
and it flew over the courtyard below,
a bag of peanuts,
and a yellow balloon someone let go.

FLOWERBUNKED

Avocados fudge
blimps to raisin
the inning, lungs
in the fatso and
braids toothpaste.
Moonlight shrugs,
star-bursting tattoo...
The popcorn village
toddlers for melted
bibs at the lip,
a boneless sniff,
snacktime in Winnipeg
duckling the mop.
When I beard, a storm
cigarettes the salad prince,
weans Amish buggy
from its horse, the poop,
and the feathered abyss
buzzes, floating beans...
Blame thick stilts. Or some
baguette-legged race
while panties melon away
hollow with Calm of Plum.

OBSOLETE TECHNOLOGIES

Bombs fall on the kisses
and the kisses wash them clean
like fruit suddenly peeled on a nice plate.

I saw the obsolete technologies,
a mop leaning on its janitor.
At midnight the prince was still a vegetable.

TAMERLANE

A fish stick is not my theme—
I will not swim that batter
Your unearthly children revelled in.

When I swim
My ripples are holy, familial.

I have not always stirred as now
The hot soup of my brow.

Hath not a chunk of earth given
A worm to a hill—this to be free?

Know thou the laundromat of a spirit
Bowed from its white sheet into stain...

It was in thy backyard I learned to whistle;
The huge thick hose of a caterpillar
Assisted my melody.

And then my whistling interrupted
The quiet of a young nun
And levelled a forest of wisdom—
O Whistle of Hell!
No hell shall wear my mouth again.

RAIN

My wet corridor dream come true was
Oh god I wanted to wipe my nose across your sleeve!
The long embarrassment paused in sleep.

When my aerosol instrument ejected a string
A leash you tugged while batting your eyes
You seemed like I meant something
But the biggest corner of the room was meant for your arms
To backstroke into its distance.

Now I see less than what I couldn't see the first time
The next step vanishing into a previous one
Like feet sweeping by, dreams over the street
As the sky leans up against buildings, scraping off its weather,
Taking damage.

OBLONG MIRAGE

1

a shovel
backfires
Baby
why don't
you can
solution me
The sunset is still bulging
to bump into

2

your fear of the phlegm's opera
comes back in the recyclable package
today
which tomorrow microwaves

3

the earth retracts a tree
scraping the suburb
a lawn ornament
hurtles through the air
the addresses
ghost bedsheets
haunt the bedbugs

a large event returns home late
dispersing smell packets
by mistake

with a Heidegger machine
among the beards of Castro's compas
and the light of whispered algebra

SONNET AFTER ANTÓNIO BOTTO

Don't chop some new droopy itch!
Don't squeeze between the oatmeal by towel!
You paddles to "again" again, to the
Shrimp in you... I knew...
So plug behind the itch
When pants was ballet—
I'm paddling just to chop again!

If someday you shrimp by yawning
And by towel stay behind
Squeezing again for new toothpaste,
Remember: Nothing droopy when pants was ballet
Raised your paddles for good, for towel
To make you leave, then go away.

SONNET TO A CHAMBERMAID AT THE PARAÍSO INTEMPORAL

You're gone again, into the elevator
and sinking towards a different future,
one without me. I imagine the sea.
The doors open into a coral reef
and you live amid colourful fish and softly
swaying tentacles like you've always dreamed.
I barely know you and I can't swim
so we don't see each other. At night
I read or look out over the balcony
at the moon. It is like my heart, a shell
that houses the silence of a great wayward crab,
one day to be washed out
among stellar billows of soft foam
into a sea of eternal laundry.

HEART-SHAPED FLY SWATTER

I look at my shadow,
the flapping sleeves
of my oversized jacket,
the scarf kicking out behind.
I look at my hand waving goodbye
as each shadow flings away,
replaced by another
cast by the next street light.

IMPROVISED DEATH SCENE

for Hannah

The twin brothers are killing each other
having just discovered they are twin brothers
and might have lived like the other
in better circumstances.
You, meanwhile, are the mother,
wearing heels and singing your heart out
so we can see it
between one brother's knife and the next.
We sit on the edge of our assigned seats,
eyes lodged in tears
until the curtain's brought down
like your hand, reaching out
and emptying us, our hearts
tearing out of their pockets.

WEARING YOUR PANTS

I tripped over my pants while wearing yours.
— Stuart Ross, "I Tripped"

Big Step

The stairs threw themselves down to the plaza.
Your health bashed around in the making, the air
really open to breathing. We were the same
in the moral of the story; after the stepladders
were propped against the mumbling giant,
the weather let us do things again, conversations
with sunglasses on. Then those pants—remember
those pants pushed off the bottom of a lake?
The water gave them a standing ovation.

Sheet Music

The opposite shore
used to sit here, nibbling
on the latest, going
brown beige pink.
The background won't
talk, a cough mounted
behind a glass sheet.
I sit at the piano.
Before playing, unfold
a napkin on my lap.

Escarpment

This walk the escarpment fills, like a shoehorn, tapering off. Later, it's brighter, as if rising in a plastic tub of light. Reaching back, there aren't enough pictures, and more lost day by day. When the postcard finally arrives, time's been carted away, wiggle room in the apartment. But standing at the edge of your feet again, no ground to count the footsteps, everything's cast in a grey blur. Is there enough where that came from? You remembered how it is. A long time. A little.

One Side of the Day

The hour pulls
to one side of the day.
Waits it out.

Shouting Our Names

I shouted your name
through a hairdo blocking my view.
You shouted my name
over the honk of a peacock.
The owner of the diner lifted a doughnut
and held it to the light, a soft blending
of pink and blue. I shouted your name
through the doughnut. You shouted back
through a long pipe stuffed with sponges
and I didn't hear you. A flowerpot
fell over. The song in our heads
was slowing down. When
it stopped, we stood
in an overgrown field
and took a bow.

Self-Portrait in Two Colours

1

A saxophone is picked up and admired.
On the next floor, nail clippers.
Spare parts are released into the wild.
The flowers flicker and bleep.

2

When the depth of field accumulates
like a landscape learning how to fill space,
a windmill sits against the early morning light
with prizes strapped to its rotating sails.

Sleeping with Myself in a Dream

There was a cough here
before taking me away.
The surgery left me stranded
on a long embarrassment
since I last wore pants.
Or from a dream of pants.
Maybe of pants.

This Chair and the Sitting That Happens In It

I wake up that morning as much as anybody. In the landscape above my head, the rules are made up again. Light stacks on a shelf, the horizon, and turning over burns another side. What makes it easier is pretending. When that falls short, a dial tone, a flicker in time with who's there, who isn't there. When the outline is visible, your name changes itself to a different spelling, a box of loose breath.

Big Step

As a visitor you will have great physical attributes
so please hear me out. The house
has lots of rooms all ending with corners
that send the walls in surprising directions.
Loose floorboards like to trade places.

To answer your question: Yes
this toe always faces that way
and this toe got frostbite.
I went a day with no colours.
The light in my head, wasting for them.

Wearing Your Pants

The sunset's gone glug,
earlids stretched
like chewing gum.
I couldn't figure out
does the music ask me
to do something?
A street light grew
like the trees around it,
different limbs
depending on the dance.

THE NEXT ARRANGEMENT OF MOLECULES

The Shadow of a Wedding Cake

moves through the courtyard
leading me to a bigger shadow
of the same wedding cake.

The Planet's

an egg balanced on a seal's nose,
children screaming in the bleachers.

Fossil

A bacterium hurtling into a pocket of pure energy
Mashed like a pie thrown into a face of pure clownness.

Another Ghostship

Grimy overalls hoist the children
Across another ghostship
An illusion bathing in the parrot's plumage
Frazzled by a long, low horn
Announcing the passing of another ghostship.

Flip Side Effects

An apple takes a bath in a painting.
The dog bares its blue woof.
Refreshments are served in the upper molars.
Finally I dissolve on my own tongue.

After Dark

smoke rises behind me
like an assassin
disguised as smoke

After the Rain of Feathers

sliced through the cathedral of smoke,
I rode my bicycle along the wharf
and watched the sun's unusual flower
settle like a duck on the lake.

The Meadow of Dents

Light slams the flowers on its way out.

The Next Arrangement of Molecules

A sheet of tiny hooks sweeps over the shrubbery
In a kind of unintentional berry-picking.

Personal Story

Electric soap drizzled around the orifice
Recharging my bald-headed pâté
Before I followed you into the bathrobe
Thus fracturing your left tibia.

At the Peak of Mt. Murder

the yo-yo panorama looks out gently
then returns, tinged with blood.

Sleeves of Wind

He moved closer to the bathroom and got "the squeaks"
Sleeves of wind functioning not unlike bicycle pumps
It occurred with many vibrations through our feet.

Selections from the Haunted House

The garden shuffles its flowers about...
Cement walls move through the grass,
bordering a cat... Mud congregates
around the sink... The floor rushes up
at a mug, smashing it across the table...
A knob turns its door off the hinges...

After Dark

the night slips into a black dress
designed for something twice its size

Kiss My Corpse

(kiss my corpse and guitar will bloom across your lips everything you say good song about kissing my corpse!)

Unchained Melody

Behind again with the monthly payments,
the molecules parted ways.

In the Atmosphere

of headlight beams and floral bedsheets,
voices trade hellos
from faces turning shyly away.

Once Upon a Time

The lovers eject their kisses,
money embezzled from a fairy tale,
over the open slopes of Montmartre.

The Next Arrangement of Molecules

At the door,
Larger than the door, now
Leaving because it can't get in.

Lunchtime

Lunchtime branches out:
a late August mid-afternoon meatloaf
among the leaves.

The New Baby

she taught me
          this. she'd say, now this and turn it that way
things like that.

The Works

Libby stamped out the adoring fists with her good foot.
Giorgio walked backwards into the eighteenth century singing
          apocryphal hymns.
Marguerite tripped over the still life and died of a surfeit of cherries.
Lemi unfurled her long body over the napping waves.
Jenny's door knocked itself out.
The hat evacuated Tom and they both ululated.

The Next Derangement of Molecules

Both my hands that are mine
will proceed to the front of your neck
and strangle it there.

Yankee Doodle

A boy with a violin showed up
who thanked me for stealing it
and left. I knew just one tune
but didn't play it. Then I played it
twice.

The Giant

She stepped away from
where her foot had been
towards the place it would be.

Wet Kiss

Spinning out from under the lips that assembled it
Before crashing into a lamppost.

The Next Arrangement of Molecules

When they found her among the bamboo,
some turquoise just above her upper lip,
it was pure sky had made a home there.

Irresistible

The demonized snare baby is impacting!
The yarn thump is backing into a furnace!
The cute reflex is falling through a sock!
O nunnery whose watering re-enacts the flowers!
O brewery whose pulsating discs vulcanize the chirpy!

The Great Tradition

I climb a ladder amid flames,
recite lines, weep decorative tears
as an ambulance wails in the great tradition of emergencies.

Reminder

Sometimes I would remember the reason
I forget about it. So
I leave you to guard the bathtub.

I'VE LIVED A LONG, PAMPERED LIFE

CHEERLESS AND READY FOR LOVE

I had come to the moat, the silent ducks.
I had dreamed of women wearing dirndls.
I have halts and starts, sobs and silences.
I have misrepresented myself.
I like horsey-backs and water balloons.
I like a curtain covering the shower stall.
I like bugs clinging to my socks.
I like the dog guiding me, carrying a lantern
on a stick in its mouth.
I met Sieghilde on rollerblades
in the cool wide corridor of a monastery,
in a lonely time among hatching silkworms,
in the garden of von Utzschneider's factory,
in the fiery trajectories of cannonballs,
in May amid the airborne beetles,
in the ricochet, the criss-cross,
in spite of the receding cliff face,
in thick shadows filling the aisles between shelves,
in getting right the hell out of there—
Sieghilde doesn't care. She hates
manoeuvring around my revolving
rack of books. I hate her collections
of opera programmes, ceramic ducks,
and circumcision knives. I have tried
to meet her halfway. She has tried
to meet me halfway. I have chopped
an onion. She has left me a note:
Meet me in the garden of the textile factory.
Meet me under the radiant moon.
Meet Yo-yo, this dog, who will guide you there,

and when you're there, meet me
in a sidelong glance,
in words that dodge the burning lips
as we watch the wolves walk on their hind legs
and the pigs squeal across the Schlossplatz.

THE SONG OF JERÓNIMO DE CAMPOS

The long shoulder
Of this "sin" flower aches
With nervous desire. Then
The morning is still far away.

The too-many-too-near arms
Come down with night,
An endless garage door
Rolling shut.

The shed in the backyard
Of your eyes... It is
My only storage solution.

ALL DIRECTIONS

Some insects learned to make holes
in the trees by spinning on their heads
and the trees turned blue at night
with the moon shining through them.
A dog barked in all directions.
Friends of the dog barked back,
and in the distance, friends of friends.

FOR NELSON

Sun
all day

yellow
balled

into
a fist

now
this

loose
rain

THE EXPERIMENT

It’s non-reflective glass. The power drill is cordless.
The bulldog has undergone a vocal cordectomy.
The zippers have been replaced with metal flaps,
which works better. The tubes are just in case.

We don’t like to use the word *secure*, but it is.
If you yawn uncontrollably, hold your nose.
If you forget when to exhale, listen deeply.
Don’t move your eyes. They’ll ruin it.

Here are the terms and conditions. Choose any three.
Here is Ben. He lived a preening and predatory youth
but now he is old and has mastered the terza rima.
His voice will guide you throughout.

Keep your hands up. Move your head to the side.
If you feel a small pinch, it’s not working. Restart.

THE VEGETAL WIDOW

the bulging stare
of earth's lap sprouts
the vegetal widow.

she flees through the
night's rag machine,
thighs rattling, hooves
licked by the ground
of ground-up glass.

what she does
most of the day is
inconspicuously
stuff corpses into
her pockets,
mocking the vultures.

SONNET FOR COW AT SUNSET

On the table, the milk
is thick and inattentive,
remembering the cow
we forget. On the wall
the echoes are erased
by more complaints,
an endless tongue that
sure as hell wants out
its mouth. The mouth
tells itself losing can be
good, doesn't hurt much,
but each morning's
removed, each night split
right down the middle.

BLOOD VENDETTA

1

A heaviness
covered the face with
hands and sobbed.

A whitish, ropelike scar ran
across the soldiers
a leftover from their days
as a Chechen woman

the quiet gave
a gentle twist.
with ant light-headedness
eyes stared like little pistons

a dark stain spread over the fabric
in ragged gasps

grey slacks and red ties stood in the middle of the lobby
They stepped into the reception
wood. the sky
shed its parachutes

2

A moron
edged along the building's exterior
Just as he did, he spotted a pair of hard-ons

a nasty grin
          snapped into place
"I'll kick the pockets off
          your pants, little mister."

a punch in the face like
          a sandwich of
hammers

3

          a choke
dawned on the
          throat.
the only way out was a place
          on the carpet behind some knees.

a minute's ritual
          bruising to its
conclusion
          the face collapsed like
a nostril-flaring towel

4

"Somewhere last week
          an occurrence conveyed
the impression of a murder."

          (fingers jabbing
                    at the air between
          the aisles)

"The victim was murdered
        by certain facts of life."

        (the envelope's flap
                held closed by a drawing of
        a man and woman locked in passion)

"Whatever feelings I had,
        the idea was peaceful melancholy,
but it lives and moves."

        (an explosion rips through
                several feet in the air
        before it turns on its side
                and takes a nap)

UNFARMILIAR

Chicken sunlight
pecks at broken glass.

Milkthirsty tailors
cut new corridors
in the cow.

A violent yoghurt
through the berries.

REAL OXYJEN

Severe reactions:
    goat breathing
    watershed in the chest
    Guatemala of the mouth

The guts uphill from the colon:
    a mop salami voyage
    floating clumps
    elastic paradise to the cactus

A Zeus overview on air remedies:
    a tahini sirocco
    the runny slash of ballet
    parade sauce of the mist

FIVE-PRONGED POEM

An archaeologist
incorrectly tastes the sandwich
like a fistful of teeth. “Well,
you can’t blow air
in your own mouth,” he whispers,
spit galloping over the sand...

The banjo did a nice thing—
now you never hear the end of it. "Where's
my noodle bonus?" sings
a thick melody
marinating in a line dance
of teriyaki sauce...

"Where's my chop and potato?"
asks the blanket over the
take-off-your-underwear bubble bath,
the overfed bulging parts
babying each other,
brown tinsel trailing behind...

The ass lumplings refuse to budge
so Dr. Nesbitt invents
the Sitting Method, a new way
to swallow involving a chest of drawers
and rapid fanning. "After I'm done,
you'll never be in the way
of what's behind you..."

Cops burst in, pants ablaze. One steps
backwards onto the escalator
of worms in an apple. "I've lived
a long, pampered life," says
the popping noise, growing
a belly before dying peacefully...

THE CLARITY OF THE SIMPLE PRESENT

Coffee keeps me awake. Riddles keep me awake. Shame
and sex keep me awake. Hunger, or that empty feeling
like hunger, keeps me awake. Indigestion keeps me awake.
A toothache keeps me awake, the black vertical line of it.
The ringing of total silence keeps me awake. Small noises
keep me awake, dramatize my paranoia: the thought of a shadow
under the door, the doorknob turning, etc., ending with me dead.
Me dead keeps me awake. Me alive keeps me awake. My eyes
keep me awake—I close them. My eyelids keep me awake—I look
beyond them into questions seductively posed at the vanguard
of human consciousness, like What is human consciousness?
An awareness of self? A road to the self? A bridge to the self?
Something said by Descartes? Something said by my dad?
Something said by a rabbit? A dying rabbit? There is a rabbit
that keeps me awake. It appeared in a poem. The rabbit leaps
and a bullet enters its brain. There is a bullet that keeps me awake.
It appeared in a dream. The bullet leaps across a yawn between
your lips, black on maroon. There is a jolt of electricity. A heart
beats. The rabbit leaps. My body is released into the delta of night
and the cold keeps me awake. The plunge. That falling
in falling asleep keeps me awake. The soundless jerk of muscle.

L'ESTASI DELL'ORO

The landscape
leaves its horizon
for a new hero.

GOING HOME

The island folded into a postcard
Banana catapult of yellow
The snap and roll of summer
In the year of the Great Tidal Crunch
It was very very close and appeared huge.

A NIGHTMARE ON PIGS, POKER, AND HEARTS

A litter of gambling pigs. I join their
poker game. Five-card draw. Show
your cards. I lose. I lose to a pair of
sixes. Hearts. The winning pig grins,
shows its teeth. I pounce. I gut the pig,
watch it smoke. A dark colour is my
heart. A dark colour is my heart. She
presses her hands over my ears and nods.

WAKING UP

From all sides
the roosters combine
the dawn with
a stolen password
like this one here
engraved on a
silver toothpick
                                        You
reach across the
table past the
toothpick past
the table
                        I slide
out from under
my dishwasher
tattoo leaving
you in the
kitchen

SONNET FOR NOUNS AT SUNSET

Boxing glove shoos away butterfly.
Hummingbird advances on teenager's pimple.
Pants around ankles shimmy back up.
Slinky scales cliff.

Mosquito plows into soap bubble.
Office chair stares at minute hand.
Candleglow bursts from pile of sand.
Buried treasure sweats.

I eat burritos with chopsticks.
I floss with film reels.
I carve hieroglyphs on bars of soap.
I attack boring gardens with tweezers.
I pick my nose and sniff gazebos.
Then I sneeze amid the swans.

INFINITE DIGESTION

How come when I bang empty the piggy bank
there's broken pretzels? Why's my pocket
full of mud? There's a mountain in the distance
pulls down its avalanches. There's an engine
makes a car go. There's a tired fly
on the windowsill. There's lime carpeting
makes me feel at home. There's the moon
a bit more to the left than usual
or is it my eyeballs a bit more to the right?
Every toy leers down from the shelf,
their batteries dead, my neighbour
pissing through the fence onto my lawn.
Cosmic dust clogs up the atmosphere,
the wind slams blossoms to the ground.
Let's fill the piggy bank with bacon bits.
Let's dance in ever-tighter circles. When I throw
this javelin at the neighbour's blow-up pool,
the water will rush out and my roses grow.
I'll hold one up to the moon, the night's nostril,
my feet lifting off as the world takes a whiff.

THE LAST ADVENTURE OF IGLI MARKU

The murdering toothpicks
hid inside the cigarettes like maypoles,
milkmaids of tobacco
skipping around as he inhaled
flesh, the tired fury of
one of the milkmaids
bravely snuck off towards the red highway
and his unusually swollen
time zone still mattered to inexistence,
an innocent pollution vacuuming the
extra eyelid the candlelight wedged between
or September fell out that day,
sneaking through autumn's long corridor of
blood, the spurting witness, and a procession
of June bugs over his turfgrassed neck
looked into the earth, saw 3 million years
including his shrivelled-up
leaving a trail of feces
so the injected molehills grew fingernails until
the foreign planet resembled a shoebox
but whether shoes
"His lips uh moved
snatched from behind flames
when suddenly a tumultuous wave of whirring agony exploded
in violent crescendos.

THE WATER CYCLE

A fat boy squatting in a blue loincloth
fades into a naked girl
who does tremendous backflips through the air
before rolling down a mountain
wrapping herself in the river's blue loincloth
becoming the boy again.

THERE IS A GRAVESTONE LIKE A DUCK

So maybe it floats in a pond
or quacks occasionally
or is shaped like a duck.
Maybe children throw crackers at it
and run away crying
as it waddles after them,
or maybe it just leaves them be
and does other things
or nothing.
It probably does nothing
though I can't be sure.
A dead thing is funny that way.

TRIPTYCH

Please go see is my cat in the house.
I worry will it rain.
Then my cat gets rained on.

*

This is my daughter, Noodles.
Stand at her left elbow
And watch the arm shoot upward
Scattering the cowardly stars.

*

Hey, human drifting in the Variation Chamber.
I push this pin through your potato.

THING HAPPENS TO ME

As the sun sinks
below city life
the last yellow
honk of light
peeks around
the edge of a
grey building
just as I turn
the corner and all
I remember next
is light squatting
over my darkness
(the evil in me)
a terrific grunt
and I was saved.

NOTES AND ACKNOWLEDGEMENTS

Some poems from this collection have appeared elsewhere: *This Magazine, In/Words, Cadences: A Journal of Literature and the Arts in Cyprus, illiterature, The Week Shall Inherit the Verse, Cosmonauts Avenue, Wearing Your Pants* (Kalamalka Press), and *Teeth, Untucked* (Proper Tales Press).

Peter and Jane of "Learn by Doing" enjoy a more peaceful existence in the Key Words Reading Scheme, a series of children's books. "Tamerlane" takes after Edgar Poe's poem of the same name. "Flowerbunked" after Barbara Ann Kipfer's *14,000 Things to be Happy About* and the first stanza of Kenneth Koch's "When the Sun Tries to Go On." "Cheerless and Ready for Love" after Kevin Connolly's *Happyland*, Dean Young's "If Thou Dislik'st What Thou First Light'st On" and W. G. Sebald's *The Rings of Saturn*. "Blood Vendetta" after Mark Laba's *The Mack Bolan Poems*, Tim Tresslar's The Executioner #409 and Ron Padgett's Creative Reading Technique No. 2: Alternate Lines. "L'Estasi dell'Oro" takes its title from a song of the same name composed by Ennio Morricone. "Oblong Mirage" from a flowerhorn cichlid of the same name at Restaurant Bamboo Bleu (flowerhorn named by Christine Miscione). "Real Oxyjen" from a collaborative family effort while on holiday, an anagram of alphabet blocks that originally read "Relax Enjoy." Phrases in "Real Oxyjen" are pulled from a series of online articles on cholesterol by Group Winew. "In the Altai Region of Russia" is from an online news headline (source defunct). "After Some New European Poets" is indebted to the first 150 pages of the anthology *New European Poets*, edited by Wayne Miller and Kevin Prufer.

Thank-yous to: Stuart Ross, for his inspiring commitment to the adventure of poetry, generosity in friendship, and as an editor, "knowing only kindness must be shown to words" (David McFadden).

Denis De Klerck, for taking on my work and the greater work of Mansfield Press. Ally Fleming and Claire Macdonald, for proofreading with care. Carolyn Smart, for her encouragement, her belief. Stephanie Bolster, Judith Herz, Mary di Michele, Sina Queyras and Gail Scott, for challenge and inspiration during my graduate degree at Concordia University. Sarah Burgoyne and Michael Casteels, for talk, camaraderie, and collaboration—I'm immensely grateful. The Fellowship of Godwitch Hall, for always listening to and reading my work with interest and sensitivity. Maggy and John of La Formule Espresso Bar, for a poet-friendly space, afternoons of writing and revising, from my first Toarco to the last Red Bourbon. Freeman Lin, for speedy photo-editing wizardry. My sister Anna, for her future choreographing of "Unfarmiliar." My sister Melina, for accompanying me on the chairlift to hell in Whistler, B.C.

Nick Papaxanthos was born in Vancouver and grew up in Lefkosia, Cyprus. He completed an undergraduate degree at Queen's University in Kingston, Ontario, where he also co-edited a comedy newspaper and gigged with a jazz quartet. In 2014, he was awarded the John Lent Poetry/Prose Award for *Wearing Your Pants*. He now lives in Montreal, a recent graduate of Concordia University's Creative Writing MA program. *Love Me Tender* is his first book.

OTHER BOOKS FROM MANSFIELD PRESS

Poetry

Leanne Averbach, *Fever*
Tara Azzopardi, *Last Stop, Lonesome Town*
Nelson Ball, *In This Thin Rain*
Nelson Ball, *Some Mornings*
Gary Barwin, *Moon Baboon Canoe*
George Bowering, *Teeth: Poems 2006–2011*
Stephen Brockwell, *Complete Surprising Fragments of Improbable Books*
Stephen Brockwell & Stuart Ross, eds., *Rogue Stimulus: The Stephen Harper Holiday Anthology for a Prorogued Parliament*
Diana Fitzgerald Bryden, *Learning Russian*
Alice Burdick, *Flutter*
Alice Burdick, *Holler*
Jason Camlot, *What The World Said*
Margaret Christakos, *wipe.under.a.love*
Pino Coluccio, *First Comes Love*
Marie-Ève Comtois, *My Planet of Kites*
Dani Couture, *YAW*
Gary Michael Dault, *The Milk of Birds*
Frank Davey, *Poems Suitable to Current Material Conditions*
Pier Giorgio Di Cicco, *The Dark Time of Angels*
Pier Giorgio Di Cicco, *Dead Men of the Fifties*
Pier Giorgio Di Cicco, *The Honeymoon Wilderness*
Pier Giorgio Di Cicco, *Living in Paradise*
Pier Giorgio Di Cicco, *Early Works*
Pier Giorgio Di Cicco, *The Visible World*
Salvatore Difalco, *What Happens at Canals*
Christopher Doda, *Aesthetics Lesson*
Christopher Doda, *Among Ruins*
Glen Downie, *Monkey Soap*
Rishma Dunlop, *The Body of My Garden*
Rishma Dunlop, *Lover Through Departure: New and Selected Poems*
Rishma Dunlop, *Metropolis*
Rishma Dunlop & Priscila Uppal, eds., *Red Silk: An Anthology of South Asian Women Poets*
Ollivier Dyens, *The Profane Earth*
Laura Farina, *Some Talk of Being Human*
Jaime Forsythe, *Sympathy Loophole*
Carole Glasser Langille, *Late in a Slow Time*
Suzanne Hancock, *Another Name for Bridge*
Eva HD, *Perfect Rotten Mouth*
Jason Heroux, *Emergency Hallelujah*
Jason Heroux, *Memoirs of an Alias*
Jason Heroux, *Natural Capital*
John B. Lee, *In the Terrible Weather of Guns*
Jeanette Lynes, *The Aging Cheerleader's Alphabet*
David W. McFadden, *Abnormal Brain Sonnets*
David W. McFadden, *Be Calm, Honey*
David W. McFadden, *Shouting Your Name Down the Well: Tankas and Haiku*
David W. McFadden, *What's the Score?*
Kathryn Mockler, *The Purpose Pitch*
Leigh Nash, *Goodbye, Ukulele*
Lillian Necakov, *The Bone Broker*
Lillian Necakov, *Hooligans*
Peter Norman, *At the Gates of the Theme Park*
Peter Norman, *Water Damage*
Natasha Nuhanovic, *Stray Dog Embassy*
Catherine Owen & Joe Rosenblatt, with Karen Moe, *Dog*
Corrado Paina, *The Alphabet of the Traveler*
Corrado Paina, *Cinematic Taxi*
Corrado Paina, *The Dowry of Education*
Corrado Paina, *Hoarse Legend*
Corrado Paina, *Souls in Plain Clothes*
Stuart Ross et al., *Our Days in Vaudeville*
Matt Santateresa. *A Beggar's Loom*
Matt Santateresa, *Icarus Redux*
Ann Shin, *The Last Thing Standing*
Jim Smith, *Back Off, Assassin! New and Selected Poems*
Jim Smith, *Happy Birthday, Nicanor Parra*
Robert Earl Stewart, *Campfire Radio Rhapsody*
Robert Earl Stewart, *Something Burned on the Southern Border*
Carey Toane, *The Crystal Palace*
Aaron Tucker, *Punchlines*
Priscila Uppal, *Sabotage*
Priscila Uppal, *Summer Sport: Poems*
Priscila Uppal, *Winter Sport: Poems*
Steve Venright, *Floors of Enduring Beauty*
Brian Wickers, *Stations of the Lost*

Fiction

Marianne Apostolides, *The Lucky Child*
Sarah Dearing, *The Art of Sufficient Conclusions*
Denis De Klerck, ed., *Particle & Wave: A Mansfield Omnibus of Electro-Magnetic Fiction*
Salvatore Difalco, *Mean Season*
Paula Eisenstein, *Flip Turn*
Sara Heinonen, *Dear Leaves, I Miss You All*
Christine Miscione, *Carafola*
Marko Sijan, *Mongrel*
Tom Walmsley, *Dog Eat Rat*
Corinne Wasilewski, *Live from the Underground*

Non-Fiction

George Bowering, *How I Wrote Certain of My Books*
Denis De Klerck & Corrado Paina, eds., *College Street–Little Italy: Toronto's Renaissance Strip*
Pier Giorgio Di Cicco, *Municipal Mind: Manifestos for the Creative City*
Amy Lavender Harris, *Imagining Toronto*
David W. McFadden, *Mother Died Last Summer*
Deborah Verginella, ed., *Bon Appetito Toronto!*

For a complete list of Mansfield Press titles, please visit mansfieldpress.net